Advan

"Virtual training today complicated. Don't you just wish someone would create a list for you to follow, to make sure nothing is missed? Well, Patricia Regier has done just that with The Online Shift. She provides advice for every step of the virtual classroom journey, including how to market your event, how to get your participants excited, and how to design your presentations. If you are looking for a quick-start guide, this is it."

—**Jennifer Hoffman**, InSync Training Founder, Author of Blended Learning, and Board of Directors Member for International Accreditors for Continuing Education and Training (IACET)

"The Online Shift is a wonderful read for anyone who is engaged in online teaching. It is filled with strategies, Hot Bonus Tips, and thoughtful approaches. It was a purposeful and enjoyable read that is relevant for novice and expert online educators alike. There are many great nuggets of information."

—**Dr. Mary Gene Saudelli**, Author of The Balancing Act: International Higher Education in the 21st Century, Associate Dean and Education, Community Development Faculty at University of the Fraser Valley

"Patricia says, 'We don't have to be perfect, we just have to try something we have never done before.' In the daunting world of virtual everything, for meetings, this one-stop-shop guide will level your game up to expert in no time. Such a valuable resource for trainers, managers, and speakers alike."

—**Tyler Hayden**, Motivational Keynote Speaker, Team Building Expert, Virtual Keynote Speaker and Bestselling Author

"This book is the ONLY book you will need to make your online presence powerful. A Must Read! My company has been fortunate to have seen Patricia's expertise in action. To have her wisdom at my fingertips, is a gift. I love how she shares her experiences, which are ones we all have had or scared to have online and then gives counsel on how to skillfully be online. This book is a must have in my resource library."

—**Kanchan Prinsloo** MA, PCC, Founder
of KaPri Consulting, Executive Coach, and
Leadership Development Principa

"The Online Shift is the must-have book every Coach, Facilitator, and Leader needs to have within arms reach as their go-to resource through the pandemic and post-pandemic virtual world! The Online Shift is the perfect compilation of everything needed to take a Coaching and Training business online! Pro tip after pro tip, chapter by chapter, and Hot Bonus Tips too, you will find yourself saying "Thank you, Patricia," over and over again as you read through this book. Patricia Regier inspires me to be the best-prepared coach and trainer I can be, and with The Online Shift, she sets me up with the tools and tips to bring that inspiration online.!"

—**Lesley Calvin** MA CPC PCC, Life, Leadership, and
Organizational Coach, Facilitator, and Speaker

"Patricia Regier was the technical director for my virtual book launch event, and I could not have done it without her! Her technical mastery ensured a stress-free and fun event. And now Patricia's written a concise, easy-to-read, and comprehensive guide on how to master your own virtual events. Covering everything from planning events to engaging audience members, this one-stop reference guide has you covered. The Hot Bonus Tips sprinkled throughout offer great gems of wisdom, and the summary list of 101 Quick Pro Tips serves as a fabulous reference tool. As a virtual facilitator, I know I'll be referring back to The Online Shift time and time again."

—**Michael Kerr,** International business speaker and author of The Humor Advantage and The Jerk-Free Workplace

"Patricia Regier's The Online Shift is a collection of personal anecdotes shared to guide marketing, designing, and facilitating online workshops. Her just-in-time collection centers the necessity of creating safe and comfortable learning spaces while improving presence and actively engaging learners. As these commitments are central to our programs, I am delighted that she has found a pathway to leverage the foundational values of her graduate education in her own professional practice."

—**Dr. Ellyn Lyle** PhD, Yorkville University, Dean, Faculty of Education

"Engaging and involving all participants in virtual meetings goes far beyond uploading slides and speaking to the screen. Patricia has shared incredible ideas and insights that let you go above and beyond what is normally expected when meeting or presenting virtually. The interactive, relevant and useful tools allow presenters to connect more fully with their audiences, promote inclusivity, and create tons of value. If you implement even a few of these ideas into your virtual meetings, you'll be way ahead of the curve.

—**Suzannah Baum**, Presentations & Leadership Communications Specialist, Executive Speech Coach

"The transition to virtual facilitation brings many challenges, and the pressure to engage is multiplied. The way we design and manage online workshops requires a 360 view of the client experience and a consistent effort to engage and align. Patricia delivers on her promise by bringing into our attention best practices and quick recovery from possible challenges and intervention. Her focus on the client experience is brilliant. The examples she offers are indispensable. Well done, Patricia!"

—**Dr. Loubna Noureddin**, EdD, PCC, Co-Founder of MindMarket, President of the International Coach Federation SF Chapter, and Executive Coach

"My favourite tip is Enable Follow Host Order. I didn't know it was possible to rearrange the order of everyone's tiles. And, to have others have my same layout is brilliant! I like the easy-to-read nature of the book. 101 tips feels easy to jump to a part that's relevant on any given day. I appreciate Patricia's stories – both her successes and failures. It's through our failures and other's that we learn the most."

—**Hannah Brown**, Award-winning Learning Design Strategist, Founder of Performance Matters

"Shifting our attitude on the ways we approach virtual training is key to effectiveness. Attitudes change with successful online learning experiences. Patricia's Regier's straight forward guide, The Online Shift, give us just what we need to create positive, successful, and engaging online learning experiences for everyone!"

—**Kassy LaBorie**, The Original Virtual Training Hero and Principal Consultant at Kassy LaBorie Consulting

THE ONLINE SHIFT

101 PRO TIPS
FOR VIRTUAL FACILITATORS

PATRICIA REGIER

To request permissions, contact the publisher at info@lifetopaper.com.

Paperback: 978-1-7780111-5-3
Ebook: 978-1-7780111-6-0

First paperback edition

Edited by Tabitha Rose & Flor Ana Mireles
Layout & Cover art by Life to Paper Publishing

Printed in the USA.
1 2 3 4 5 6 7 8 9 10

Life to Paper Publishing Inc.
Canada | U.S.A.

www.lifetopaper.com

CONTENTS

DEDICATION PAGE

This book is sincerely dedicated to all my clients and colleagues, who have asked for my advice and trusted me to support them these past couple of years! *You* shifted to the online context with courage and make me proud! Some of you shifted to this new virtual world with hesitation, but you did it and *are* doing a great job! Thank you to all of you who said that you couldn't wait to read this book.

I also dedicate this book to my husband and daughters, who encouraged me and are just as thrilled as I am to be publishing my first book. Thank you to all my family and friends who are celebrating this with me.

The lines can blur between the following sections, but if you consider these quick pro tips when planning your learning experience, you are then designing for the best results for the online shift. For your ease, you can see the checklist of all 101 quick pro tips used throughout at the end of this book.

INTRODUCTION

Facilitating workshops and learning experiences online can be fantastic, but it is ever-changing and requires a virtual approach. I planned to publish this book as everyone was experiencing The Online Shift, during the year of the great pivot. I was perfectly positioned to share my knowledge about online facilitation, but became very busy helping speakers, leaders and facilitators to embrace the new virtual context. And I am glad that I waited to share these quick pro tips with the world.

I have had the privilege to work with hundreds of amazing clients who had to move their in-person workshops to the digital space. The quick tips list grew as I saw what the needs were, including the missteps fantastic facilitators were making. The online context is different. I am very impressed with how facilitators embraced the learning curve and have had confidence to embrace the online shift.

Walking alongside facilitators, speakers and organizations as they had to quickly change or shift the way they shared content. Equipping facilitators to feel great about their new online training space is very rewarding! This book is dedicated to all of you! You are brave, you are talented, and you have done a fantastic job shifting your content online. Here are quick pro tips, so that you can facilitate engaging virtual learning experiences!

This book is for: Online facilitators, workplace trainers, and speakers who already have or will shift workshops and training online. Maybe you are thinking of expanding your virtual or digital training options, or you had to move online but want to improve the experience for yourself and your participants. If you want to turn your online presentation audience into participants, then this book is for you.

WHO I AM

My name is Patricia Regier, and I am passionate about creating online learning experiences that aren't boring for the participants and are enriching for the facilitator. My qualifications include a Master of Adult Education and over twenty years of experience creating and facilitating learning experiences in the workplace, academic settings and in the community. I have over ten years of experience leading and participating in online learning. I also truly get excited when there is a new update in Zoom, or when I have learned a new multimedia application tool that I can apply to facilitation.

My mission is to help learning and development professionals, speakers and facilitators feel confident in the online, virtual, and digital training space. Since technology keeps shifting, it brings facilitators opportunities to enhance great content and lead engaging learning. My vision is to turn audiences into participants by facilitating meaningful online learning experiences.

HOW TO USE THIS BOOK

Do you buy books and feel almost like you are collecting them; planning to read them on a day that you are less busy? You are buying the book because you need help with the topic, but you don't always get around to reading it. Well, this book is designed to be an easy, on-the-go book. You can read one section or skip ahead, choosing your own adventure, depending on what quick pro tips you need at the moment. Continue to use this book as your *just-in-time* resource, as you **shift** workshops and facilitation **online**. Go back to a section to see what you have checked off, and what you have not read or tried yet.

This book is divided into five chapters: Promo, Preparedness, Prelude, Presence, and Promise.

[These five elements of facilitating engaging online learning experiences are also part of a self-directed online micro-course, which includes videos and downloadable resources. You'll have access to this course as a special package with this book, or you can just access one or the other.]

If you are feeling stuck about one aspect of your online learning events or don't know what is missing, this book can help. There may be aspects you had not considered, in regards to the stages of: *before* your learning event, *during* the training or *after* the experience.

This book is for online facilitators. If you lead online trainings, workshops, presentations or meetings, you can check off the steps you already take, and feel great about that! You can also see what you have yet to check off. Just pick one or two items to begin with, and you can come back to the book when you want to add another element.

My hope for you is to enjoy facilitating online and to feel confident that you are creating engaging learning experiences. The goal is for your participants to remember how great they felt when attending your event and remember your content. These quick tips will help prevent the no-shows, or drop-offs, when facilitating or shifting online. **You can do this!** And you can keep doing this (if you want or need to). Being able to thrive while facilitating online is always a great back-up option, step-in option, or intentional 'this fits my life' option.

Enjoy diving into these quick pro tips!

CHAPTER ONE

Promo: How To Promote Your Event Or Workshop

This promo, or promotion, chapter is *not* about marketing, but is instead a starting place for the learning experience journey and considering your participants. These tips include aspects of communication and are the foundation that you provide before the actual event.

💬 Promo In Practice - Jumping In

One way to build excitement and knowledge about an upcoming online workshop is to 'Go Live.' Getting on camera can feel weird, but it's a great way to record something for people to watch later—or join you live, in real time. Sometimes, when you hit that 'Go Live' button, there isn't anyone watching. One day, I found out about a new option in Zoom and I was thrilled. I hit 'Go Live' on Instagram and shared my excitement. This promoted that I was going to create a video tutorial about the new update soon and told people to stay tuned. Then, I couldn't find the 'End Live' button when I was finished, but this just added some humor and vulnerability. It's part of the magic when you are 'live' and are demonstrating the shift to online.

We don't need to be perfect. We just need to do something that we have never done before. This ongoing learning can inform how we engage our participants and it helps us understand their perspective when trying something new. The promotion of your event or the thing you are working on can build participants' readiness and learning. One person who watched that live told me later that my excitement got her excited to try out the new feature on Zoom the next time she facilitated. 'Jumping in' to share your enthusiasm, in the moment, whether you go live, press record, or write a social media post or blog, can engage your participants before they decide to sign up for your workshop.

How To Build Promotion

❑ Bring People Into A Safe, Authentic Space

Bringing people into a safe, authentic space helps them be present and ready for deeper learning. We can't always pack in as much content into an online event, but it can be meaningful and memorable. Facilitators make an impact with learning experiences designed for intentional connections. Create safe spaces that are authentic, fun and responsive to your participants' needs. Becoming a flexible facilitator, speaker and educator requires planning, knowledge and a bit of courage. You can include information in your promotion that sets the stage for the atmosphere participants can expect. Promotion communications are an important part of the learning experience journey. How people enter a learning experience, and how they join, sets them up for success. If someone does not have the event link, then they don't show up and they can't learn. If someone does not feel welcome or safe, then they won't be confident to be vulnerable and share what they don't know. These aspects can impact an openness to learning. Feeling safe also includes feeling prepared and comfortable. This is why it's important to include learning materials for how to navigate a learning platform and what to expect.

❏ Incorporate Breaks & Snacks

Help people through those longer online learning days or sessions by incorporating breaks and snack times. Make sure people know the timeline for the whole event, especially online. Providing this information ahead of time can help participants plan their day. For example, think about how much time it takes to make a lunch, or if people are sharing the internet at home, and how long do they want to ask their family to not stream movies.

❏ Be Aware Of How Engagement Impacts Learning

Do you lead meetings with your camera on or off? Do you turn on your mic to participate, when you attend an event? Do you type in the chat? We all have different ways we like to communicate and engage online. But it's important to note that engagement does impact our learning. What can also be expected, when people shift to the online context, is that they are experiencing a learning curve. Another consideration is that people may be a bit tired of the virtual context. Make decisions ahead of time and then communicate expectations. Or if you are leading a regular meeting, or learning series, create the expectations together as a group.

❑ Add A Time Zone To Your Promo Information

Don't forget to include the time zone details in your promotional materials and calendar invites. The shift to online learning experiences, events and meetings have the benefit of bringing people from across the country or around the world. Clear communication can avoid frustrations or embarrassment if people don't realize the correct time.

❑ Make An Introduction Or Welcome Video

A short introduction or welcome video can increase excitement and helps people to show up for the meeting or training. It also allows the participants to get to know you a little bit beforehand and breaks the ice. Get creative and have fun with this!

❑ Find Out What Your Participants' Needs Are

Ask before the event if anyone needs closed captions or other learning or accommodations.

❏ **Share Necessary Links And Have Your Participants Test Them Beforehand**

Send a link to your participants to download the platform application or test it on their computer. This is best to be completed before the learning event or workshop.

❏ **Get Creative**

Get creative with your pre-event promotion and information. Set the stage that your participants are going to enjoy the learning!

❏ **Create A Pre-Survey**

Do you need a learning needs or gaps assessment for your group? This is not a test, but can instead enable you to customize the content for your participants. A pre-survey can also help your group know if this training is the right fit and gets them interested in the content.

❏ **Share Bite Size Tips**

Sharing bite size tips online via social media can help grow your group and get people excited. You can share videos to LinkedIn, post on Instagram, go live on Facebook, or post something to your organization's private intranet/sharepoint.

❏ Remember Promotion Is More Than Marketing

Promotion is not just marketing. Think about promotion as the beginning of the learning experience. What will get your participants excited to participate when they arrive?

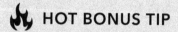 **HOT BONUS TIP**

Online experts will often talk about the 'Know, Like & Trust' factor. Going LIVE or creating short videos on the platforms where your participants are gives them a chance to get to know you, your personality, and your speciality.

CHAPTER TWO

Preparedness: What You And Your Participants Need Before They Arrive

The 'prepared' quick tips for your event or workshop will highlight what you and your participants need before they arrive. Preparation also includes aspects of communication and the next level of foundation that you are providing before the actual event, workshop or training session. These pro tips help you, as the facilitator, and the participants be prepared, especially with the online shift.

◯ **Prepared In Practice - Need For Speed**

I used to always have to kick everyone in my household off the internet when I was facilitating an online workshop to protect my internet speed. I would have my computer connected with an ethernet cable, but sometimes my video or sound would grabble, which really interrupted the flow of the experience. When people said that I froze, I had to repeat the content, or they couldn't see the video because it was buffering, it was frustrating for everyone involved.

A couple of years ago, I wanted to get certified as an online speaker through a company that was going to give me a badge. I was all set and had practiced my short talk, which they were going to record. I knew that they were also going to test my internet speed, but I thought I had the fastest internet that I could get in my area. Well, I failed that test, and it was awful because this is what I do for my work. I remember thinking, "What was I going to do next?"

The infrastructure in my area impacted all internet providers. I did some research and found a cable-based company. I wanted to get that badge, so I made the big leap. This was a big change because I had over 20 years of accounts with an email address that was no longer going to work. This was going to be some work if I was going to make this shift.

However, changing my internet provider was completely worth it! A 5-minute YouTube video, which used to take all night to upload, now only took a minute or two. This meant that, when I presented information, I could share a video clip and not worry that it would freeze. That 'fail' was the best thing to save me time and protect the quality of online facilitation and production services I could offer my clients. Getting prepared sometimes requires a change, a shift from how you always did things, and may include a learning curve, but it is always worth it.

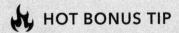

🔥 HOT BONUS TIP

You can internet search 'speed test' in order to find out how fast your internet is (wifi or ethernet cable connection). This is the math that was not on the school curriculum. There are upload Mbps (megabits per second) and download speeds. You need higher speeds for streaming video, so it won't buffer when you are sharing it to your participants.

💬 Prepared In Practice - Avoided Disaster

One day when I was getting ready to produce for a client, my modem stopped and restarted out of nowhere. This made my heart drop as I thought about what would happen if this occurred during a workshop.

I have power backup systems so that we are not interrupted, and if the internet provider has issues, I would switch over to data. However, when the internet stops, it drops me as Host. The meeting will continue with the co-host, but I didn't want to be embarrassed by the situation of the speaker not knowing how to let me back into the meeting. There was no time to call the internet provider because my facilitator was about to arrive. So, I decided to log into the meeting from my cell phone as a backup device with the data turned on. I knew this could cost me some money, but I couldn't let the worst scenario occur.

I kept the Wi-Fi on my phone, and hoped that the data would only be used if the internet dropped. Then, in the middle of the meeting. the modem stopped and then restarted AGAIN. My computers (I had a backup computer logged in, too) both got kicked out of the meeting. However, since I was logged onto my phone as a co-host, I could still let people into the meeting, and take care of my tasks.

Thank goodness I knew how to host from my phone and that no one knew about the tech issues I was experiencing, just as the meeting got started. The modem restarted right away, and after I logged back in from my computer, it made me host again. Disaster averted!

> ### 🔥 HOT BONUS TIP
>
> If you have an old phone or tablet, clear the stuff that was on it and download the apps for the online platforms you often use. If you have the passwords already set up, it's another back-up option you can use.

💬 Prepared In Practice – Participant's Perspective

It's good to log into meetings as a participant from different devices, but also different platforms. When we get comfortable as facilitators, it's hard to stay aware of other people's learning curves. However, understanding our participants' perspectives can aid us in providing them direction when they are shifting to a new platform.

I was logging into a training course on a new platform that I had never used before. A lot of skills are transferable from platform to platform so I didn't do as much research or prep. I was a participant, and when I clicked the link to join, it didn't work the way I was expecting. I then entered through the browser instead of downloading the app. When the facilitators were telling us to click the green checkmark, I didn't have that option. This was frustrating, and I was a bit embarrassed because I had not taken the time to follow all the pre-course steps. However, going through this experience reminded me of what my participants could be feeling. This was a good example of what I needed to do to support a positive start to a workshop or course for my participants.

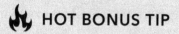 **HOT BONUS TIP**

It's good to log into meetings as a participant from different devices, but also from different platforms. When we get comfortable as facilitators, it's hard to stay aware of other people's learning curves. However, understanding our participants' perspectives can aid us in providing them direction when they are shifting to a new platform.

 **How To Prepare As A Facilitator**

❑ **Know Being Prepared Makes All The Difference In Online Facilitating**

A prepared facilitator, speaker or leader can make all the difference in preparing your participants. Intentionally set aside time to prep!

❑ Have Your Technology And Equipment Ready Ahead Of Time

If you are the facilitator or speaker, having your technology sorted out ahead of time is really important. A good-quality, working mic and camera are important to making the experience feel more like the 'in-person' context and helps people to *not* focus on the technology.

❑ Be Sure Your Internet Is Strong

Your internet strength can impact how people see and hear you. One tip for helping a poor internet connection is to use a high-speed ethernet cable and hardwire your computer to the modem instead of relying on Wi-Fi in the home. Remember, your internet determines your sound quality, which is essential.

❑ Give Your Participants Instructions

Sending video tutorials or screenshots with step-by-step instructions ahead of a meeting, for how to update a meeting platform app or how to use some of the engagement tools, can support participation. This is for your attendees, but it's also an early step of content creation and prep for a facilitator to plan for.

❑ Share And Discuss Expectations

Discussing expectations and intentionally inviting people to turn on their cameras and mics may be necessary for engagement to occur. Make sure that people know they will be muted, or they should be ready to mute themselves or turn off their camera if background noise is disruptive or distracting. Demonstrate compassion and understanding that some people may need to keep their camera and mic turned off because of a home-shared working and learning space. If you're planning on having full learning days or series, these workshops can also begin with expectation setting collaborative discussion. Including everyone ensures that people are respectful with their interactions in chat, on mic or on camera, and within breakout groups. Also, ensure that people are using a variety of communication tools, especially since they are not in person or face-to-face. Starting the day with some of these aspects is good, but sharing expectations ahead of time can also shorten the time you spend on this. Expectations can be part of your promo or the prelude, (beginning of event). As a facilitator and leader, you must first decide what your expectations and hopes are, and how you will encourage cameras on, or guilt-free cameras off.

❑ Ensure Partnering Facilitators Are Prepared

If you are working with different facilitators, speakers and leaders for a learning event, ensure they are also prepared ahead of time. Do they know how to share their slides (with sound) and everything that goes with speaking online? Do they have back-up plans if their internet goes down or their computer stops working? Will they follow the clear time-lines on the agenda outline? Discussing all of this ahead of time and scheduling a technical practice can set you *all* up for success!

❑ Have Back-Up Plans Prepared

Prepare yourself, your participants, and additional speakers or facilitators to have a back-up plan in place. If the power goes out, how will you continue to run the virtual learning experience or event? What is your back-up plan if the internet goes down? Be prepared to use the data from your phone, and ask yourself if your phone signal works at your desk. Think about alternative options for someone else to share your slides, or have a back-up computer also connected. Your context may not include all these options, but think about the 'What Ifs.' What if *this* happens…What would you do? This could even include having batteries ready for your computer mouse so you don't miss a beat.

❑ Prepare Resources For Your Participants

Send resources ahead of the meeting, and do a check-in earlier during the learning event to ensure people have the tools you provided them. If they don't, be ready to drop them into the chatbox, or another method, so that your participants get the most out of your content. Part of your prep is to make time for this in your agenda, and have a team in place for someone else to help with tech issues. With all of this prepared, you can move forward and focus on the content and the experience. [If your event includes a hybrid audience, these resources may need to be printed for those in-person and electronic for those online.]

❑ Include 'Clickable' Links

When sharing resources ahead of time or during a learning experience, consider the participants' experiences and include 'clickable' links where applicable. If people have to take additional steps to copy and paste, then they don't always do this. If there is something you want people to read or watch ahead of time or during the learning event, make it as accessible as possible, with ease and clarity. (Clickable includes a hyperlink with the http:// part.)

❑ Make Sure Your Speakers Are Ready

Before the event begins, make sure that you and your speakers are ready. Do a tech check to make sure the speakers know how to share their slides with computer sound if a video clip is embedded. Plus, letting your speakers enter into the meeting early to make sure their mic and camera is working can help them feel confident when it's time to present. This is in addition to the separate technical practice meeting. If something is not working, a quick fix can happen before the event starts.

❏ Communicate With Your Team Or Partners

If you are working with a production partner or team, communicate each person's roles and responsibilities and practice how you will work together. This can include a timeline, show notes, or a step-by-step detailed plan. Communicate in real-time if you are shortening the breakout group time, or the break. Discuss ahead of time how you want your production partner to interrupt and mention a comment or question in the chat you may have missed.

❏ Create A Timeline Or Guide

Part of your prep is to create a timeline for a learning experience. This guide should consider the technical steps occurring in the background, such as dividing up participants into specific breakout groups, while you are sharing your presentation. Providing time for you or someone else to complete this task before the event starts allows for things to flow more smoothly.

❑ Test And Update Your Technology

Test your technology and update your learning platform often. In addition, encourage and support your participants to have the most up-to-date platform.

❑ Record

Sometimes, when we try things for the first time—for example, going LIVE with a group—it's best to press record. This can be helpful for creating a tutorial video to send to your participants before the event, or can even be helpful in creating a video clip for promo. Recording your events, learning experiences, and workshops, when appropriate, can also be helpful in case you want to go back and see what you did or you have someone who couldn't make the event, but still wants to be involved. However, recording can change how people participate on camera. Consider this and communicate if you are recording.

🔥 HOT BONUS TIP

When you send a document or speaker form for an upcoming virtual event, name the form including the individual speaker name. Then, the receiver doesn't have to rename the document and you don't have to open it in order to rename. This is helpful if you have multiple speakers that you sent the same form to.

How To Prepare Your Participants

❏ Provide Support With Tools

Providing technology navigation prep support before an event with a video tutorial, downloadable checklist, or any other user-friendly tool, is a great set-up for a good learning experience for participants. Showing them how to update the online learning platform or any other technical support they need ensures they can use all engagement tools in the learning experience.

❏ Be Mindful Of Your Participants' Learning and Technical Conditions

If people cannot see or hear each other, then it is hard to collaborate. Therefore, having a working mic, camera and stable internet can help remove the barriers when technology is not working. However, we must also be aware that everyone does not always have access to a new external mic, camera, or high-speed internet. Sending tips to improve a participant's individual and collective experience can make a difference. In addition, don't make assumptions. For example, calling the number symbol "Pound" may be confusing because many people know this to now be the "Hashtag" symbol. This example is particularly important when it comes to sending promotions or communications that are meant to help people feel prepared.

❑ Ask If Accessibility Or Learning Needs Are Required

Asking participants ahead of the learning event if they need Closed Captioning, or have other accessibility and learning needs in the communications may also help engagement and it assures the participants that you care about their needs. Remove as many barriers as possible for your participants. Walk in their shoes, or, in this case, fingers and mouse clicks on their computer. Especially with accessibility and learning differences, be mindful of what additional steps you may need to take to be inclusive. This could include PDF's that can be used for text to audio and visuals that are described. (This is not a comprehensive list, but rather an important aspect to consider when designing the learning experience.)

❑ Lay Down Ground Rules

Ground rules or expectations at the beginning of a new learning day can include recommendations for the best learning experience. For example, shutting down other browser tabs improves internet strength. Another example could be establishing a 'no selling' rule. A recent client told me that she added this to her ground rules and I thought it was a smart idea for some groups, especially when they go into breakouts.

You can communicate some of this before the event as well. Other ground rules may apply to the profile pictures when someone has their camera off, which, on some platforms, can be turned off for everyone if it is an issue.

❑ Make Sure Events Get Added To Participants' Calendars

Make sure participants have a calendar invite that fits with their calendars. You can ask ahead of time if they use Outlook/Microsoft, Google Calendar, or another digital calendar. For example, if you send a Zoom link via Google, this may also include a Google Meet-up link. Having two links within an invite is confusing. If someone does not use Microsoft Outlook, and they only get an Outlook invite, they may not be able to accept it. They also have to add the link and information into their calendar system manually, and if they forget, they may not show up. Talk to a tech person for help since this may feel complicated and over-whelming, but don't skip this important detail.

❑ Add Reminders And Support Once Your Event Is Set Up

When you send the meeting link and calendar invite (compatible with all email/calendar systems), you can also have built-in and automatic reminder texts or messages, so participants can show up feeling prepared. Reminder emails are helpful because they can resend participants the link to the event the day or an hour before. However, it is good to communicate that you are providing this reminder as a courtesy (or ask permission). Let people know you are doing this to support them, not annoy or disturb them.

❑ Send The Platform's Backup Phone Number

The backup phone number is important, just in case a participant's mic or speakers stops working. With that said, when/if it is time for breakout group divisions, keep in mind that some participants may be using both their phone and computer. If that is the case, you may want to merge or send both 'gallery tiles' into the same breakout room.

❑ Make Sure Participants Have Their Documents

Make sure your participants have the documents they need ahead of time and remind them to have them available. Be prepared to drop the document into the chat box or file pod within the meeting if needed.

CHAPTER THREE

Prelude: What To Do At The Beginning Of Your Event To Get Participants Excited

The prelude is the beginning, or just before the start of an event. The prelude can be the online lobby or waiting room, or be the part just as people join the online classroom or learning space. This can be the first icebreaker or warm-up activity that you choose to get the excitement for learning started.

💬 Prelude In Practice - Breaking The Ice

I was trying what used to be an in-person ice-breaker as an adapted online version for the first time with a group. I had practiced it, prepared for it, but this warm-up activity had not been fully tested with a whole group yet. The icebreaker worked out great within this online context. I was so relieved! However, when I was explaining the instructions, through my nervous energy, I was going a little fast. All of a sudden on my PowerPoint slide, the words 'Too Fast' appeared because one of my participants was drawing it. The person didn't know everyone could see the annotation since I had just taught them how to use this engagement tool. However, we all had a good laugh (without embarrassment), which was a perfect icebreaker warm-up element. I learned what I would tweak next time for this activity, which included a sticky note on my computer, or in my notes, to slow down.

Prelude In Practice - The Silent Start

One time, when I was producing for an online keynote speaker, the hosts started by opening their meeting in the gallery view. They may or may not have had a presentation slide already shared, *but no one was saying anything*. Nothing was being typed in the chat. They were silently waiting for the hundreds of people to join the meeting before they began. The problem was that people started wondering if their own audio was not working. Questions started being asked in the chat if they should be hearing someone talk. This was not the best start! Even if you frequently have to be saying welcome (out loud on the mic), adding music, frequent messages to the chat, or even having a message on the screen that says, 'We will begin shortly,' and that you are waiting for everyone to arrive can be helpful and keep people engaged as they wait. Having a warm-up activity ready also helps to build engagement and interest. With complete silence, people can walk away from their computer to fill up their cup of coffee and miss the beginning or start of the event.

How To Manage The Prelude As A Facilitator

❏ Add Details To The Waiting Room

If your platform has an option to add details to the waiting room before people are let into the online meeting, then customize that space to make it friendly, informative and welcoming. This is the place to set the tone for your event just before it starts.

❏ Send Your Participants Friendly Messages

When you aren't ready to let people in from the waiting room just yet, send friendly messages (i.e. into the Zoom Waiting Room) acknowledging their arrival and that you are excited they are here. On some platforms, you may need to send frequent messages as more people arrive since they don't see the message sent just before they arrived. Mix up the messages, so that people who have seen every message get excited for the event and what is to come.

❑ Decide If Participants Will Join Muted Or Unmuted

When you let participants in, decide if you will have them muted upon entry and if they will have the option to un-mute themselves. Muting participants upon entry avoids the need to mute someone that does not realize that their mic is on, which also avoids embarrassing situations. Since it's frequent for events to mute upon entry, many people may assume they are muted when they enter an online meeting. If you're not planning on muting participants on entry, let them know how to mute themselves ahead of time.

❑ Have A Welcome Message Ready

Have your shared screen ready with a welcome message. This can include asking if people need Closed Captioning (CC), if this fits your context and audience. Other times, you may want to begin a small group, with everyone in gallery view, without a slide shared. Still, you should have a welcome message ready, whether it's on the screen in a slide, in the chat or you're just saying it on mic. It's uncomfortable for people to enter an online meeting with complete silence.

❑ Ask In The Chat About Closed Captioning

In addition to information on a slide and asking ver-bally, remember to ask in the chat if anyone needs Closed

Captioning. It is important to use technology for increasing engagement and inclusion. Make sure that you have this setting activated in your account (if necessary) before your meeting or event.

❏ Set The Tone With Music

You may want to open your meeting with some royalty free music to set the tone and energy level of the learning experience.

❏ Let Participants In Early

Consider letting participants in from the waiting room early. Do the tech navigation and chat before you officially begin. Did you let participants into the room to sit down and get ready before you began to train when you were in person? Don't keep people waiting; jump in with a warm-up activity! Have an activity or two ready while you are waiting for everyone to arrive, or if a speaker or facilitator is late.

❏ Consider Turning Off The Waiting Room Once It Is Time To Start

When you start the meeting or event, consider turning off the waiting room if you aren't working with a technical partner. This ensures that if someone is late, you don't miss letting them in. However, if security is a concern, you can turn the waiting room back on, depending on the platform you are using.

❏ Start With A Tech Check

Start with a technology check-in and navigation instructions so everyone starts with the same knowledge and is comfortable within the online learning context. Demonstrate with screenshots, while sharing your screen or within a slide, and explain verbally where their mic is and how they are able to mute and unmute. Explain to the participants how to turn on their camera and where to type in the chat. You can also have your production partner cover this as people enter the room before you begin.

❏ Have A Navigation Slide

A navigation slide for how to use the engagement tools is helpful for the online platform. This will ensure that everyone knows how they can participate, or alternate ways to participate. Explaining the steps for how people can navigate the next part of an activity is important because the technology may be new to some. Never assume that just because you find it easy others will too. You may do this before and/or as part of the icebreaker warm-up activity.

❑ Screen Share Your Desktop

Screen sharing your desktop is a great option to show visually what people are looking at, to explain step-by-step instructions, and help someone to navigate a platform if you don't have slides ready. You can also use screenshots, but with visuals include very specific auditory cues and steps if someone is only calling in and cannot see what you are explaining.

❑ Consider Navigation Differences

Some participants may be joining the event or meeting on different devices. Consider these navigation differences, such as Mac v.s. Windows, or phone v.s. computer.

❑ Check In On Your Participants

Ask your participants if they can hear you or see what you want them to see if your screen is shared. However, do this in a subtle way by saying, "Who here is excited for today's event? Give me a green checkmark"—or red X depending on the platform.This is a way to make sure people can hear you and get the engagement started. Just be sure to explain *how* people can find the engagement and reaction tools in the platform beforehand.

❑ Have Online Roundtable Introductions

When applicable, don't skip this part! Roundtable introductions are a great way to bring everyone into the current virtual context instead of people being distracted by other things in their physical context. This can also be your icebreaker and ask everyone what they hope to learn. If the group is small, you can do this on camera. If it's very large, then you can do this in the chat or with a poll to ignite engagement. Introductions can be a very powerful starting point for a small group that will be learning together. They give everyone a chance to contribute, and sometimes, additional prompts may be needed since some people may become less interactive in an online meeting. Introductions also warm people up to collaborative learning. If you don't do this as a large group, leave time for this in the breakout groups. Also, asking people to say their name on the mic can be a mic test and helps you know how to pronounce someone's name correctly. If you have time and if your learning experience is for team building or networking, introductions are an important aspect to consider building in.

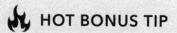 **HOT BONUS TIP**

Ask someone to say the next person's name so that you don't waste time waiting for the next volunteer.

❑ Enable Follow Host Order

Arrange the order of the video tiles for how you would like to see people. For example, you may have the panelists at the top of the gallery and then click 'Follow host order' if your platform has this capacity. This way, everyone has the same order. In some platforms you can also organize participants in alphabetical order in the 'Participants' Panel.'

❑ Make The Prelude As Inviting And Comfortable Online As It Would Be In Person

Icebreaker activities online require some technical directions, but it's important to make them inviting and comfortable for participants. Focus on the reason for the activity. Oftentimes, it's to warm up the group and set the tone for the experience.

❑ Have Fun, Relevant Warm-Up Activities

Add a fun, but relevant, activity or warm-up experience to your online workshop. A quick activity can transition people into the learning mindset, so consider picking something that encourages people to turn on their mic and camera without excluding people who can't do so. If you have many people who will be off-camera/mic, then also use check marks and the chat frequently.

❑ Have An Energizer Activity

Try an icebreaker, energizer activity, or a 'learning how to use an engagement tool' activity, even if you are doing it for the first time going Live. It's OK if it does not work out perfectly! You'll learn from the experience and then try it again. Plus, your participants benefit from you adding additional engagement. Energizer activities can also be a brain teaser or touch points, when you come back from a break, or when you are switching topics.

❑ Have A Virtual Background Icebreaker

Virtual backgrounds can become a fun icebreaker, too. You can send out a tutorial video ahead of time, or show people how to upload their own background in one session and ask them to be ready for their personalized background in the next session. This can also relate to your specific topic or content, especially if you sent out a quiz or evaluation ahead of time.

❑ Use The White Board Annotation

An icebreaker option or idea is to use the white board and annotation feature, if your platform includes this. You can often use annotation when presenting a PowerPoint slide so you don't have to stop sharing your screen. You can use similar interactive elements on platforms such as Zoom,

MS Teams, Adobe Connect and WebEx. For example, once you have your white board annotation set up, ask questions such as, "What makes online learning engaging for you?" or "What is not helpful to your learning?" and let participants type above or below the line you already have set up in the slide.

❏ Think About Purpose, Process, and Payoff

When selecting or adapting an icebreaker activity to do with participants, think about the purpose of the icebreaker, its process and how it will pay off. When shifting an activity online, make sure it works with the context, but don't drop activities just because they take another step, such as a mini navigation lesson, before running the activity.

❏ Spotlight The Speaker

Decide if you are going to spotlight the speaker. Doing so pushes the main speaker as the person who your participants see. If the learning has a team building purpose, you may want to leave it up to the participants to see speaker or gallery view, or, depending on the platform, suggest how they set up their view.

❑ Consider The Details When You Set The Stage For The Learning Experience

When you shift the learning experience or meeting online, consider as many details as you can think about from different perspectives. In person, you may have had markers and sticky notes on the tables for the warm-up activity as people entered the room. Online, consider how to shift the activities and instructions to the new context, but always keep the participants' experience in mind first.

CHAPTER FOUR

Presence: Turn Audiences Into Participants

Your presence when facilitating has one of the biggest impacts, especially online when you are trying to reach and engage participants through a computer. Your presence and tone of voice conveyed online can impact drawing in your audience. Along with other elements through the learning experience design, your enthusiasm can determine if your audience will turn into participants. Your presence can also come through the online shift, even if in a particular group or platform context everyone has their camera off.

Presence In Practice - Professional On Top

When online facilitating, presenting, giving a keynote or talk, some of my colleagues stand, even though they are at home. They get in front of cameras, put on their stage shoes, and tell me this impacts how they feel, and therefore, their presence on camera. This may be different for everyone. My set-up, with lights, a camera, a mic, a stream deck, and even props, means that I often sit when I facilitate online. I may still be wearing comfy pants, but my top is professional, and I am comfortable. My energy and excitement when facilitating comes through the computer, and people can feel it! When I started filming YouTube videos, I felt awkward and that came through the camera. However, that first feeling of being out of my comfort zone was OK because, the more I got in front of the camera, the more comfortable I became. It was the only way to improve; I had to put myself out there!

 HOT BONUS TIP

Be kind to yourself, and be intentional about using positive self-talk. You got this! You are doing great!

Presence In Practice - Eye Contact

I once had a colleague mention that she didn't connect with a person because they didn't look directly into the webcam. This is how many facilitators and participants may feel about how they connect with others online, but it doesn't have to be the case. I had another client who almost always had their camera off, but with just hearing the tone of their voice, I still felt connected and engaged in the conversation.

How do you feel about cameras being on or off? It's good to think about this for each group you work with. There are pros and cons and every context is different. Getting a break, by intentionally being 'off camera' can be really nice, but connection still needs to be established through tone of voice. Part of our presence as facilitators is to draw in the participants and build trust. We can authentically connect through the camera, or just through the speakers of our computers!

 How To Shift Your Presence For More Engagement

❏ Be Intentional

The presence participants can feel when they join a virtual training or digital workshop experience must be intentional.

Shifting events, meetings and training online can include meaningful connections, but the shift must include many of these pro tips.

❏ Energy Is Key

Your energy is key. This includes your tone and the inflection in your voice. In addition, because of the online setting, your facial expressions make a difference. So, remember to smile, even if you are not on camera. High energy is more engaging than a boring tone of voice, so make things fun— both for you and the participants!

❏ Use Props

Props are a good unexpected option to build your presence, too, especially online. You can be high-tech, low-tech, or a combination. Just add something!

❏ Make Eye Contact

Eye contact online is looking into the camera lens. Look directly into the camera as much as possible, nod your head when you are listening, and only sometimes, look at your participants' video tiles to view their body language. Eye contact online is different. If people see you always looking to the side or down, it is a very different experience. This is especially important if a meeting or training is being recorded for some people to watch as a replay.

❑ Build Connection

In order to connect with your participants online, be real, authentic, professional, and vulnerable. Connection is part of engagement, so expand the digital span of connection between you and your participants.

❑ Communicate

Like energy, communication is also key when facilitating online and when working with your support team. Check in with your participants and let your tech-support people know about any adjustments in timelines or tasks. This manages the energy in the learning experience because people are not getting frustrated with the technology.

❑ Be Present

When online facilitating, be present. Remember to pause and listen. This is extra important because we are doing so much of our communication online. We can't always see body language, movements, or even how people are breathing. Mics are often on mute—for good reason, but it changes the communication, especially when we can't always see everyone that we are training or meeting with. Making an effort to create engagement and intentionally taking time to pause and listen is crucial. One way to be present in online events is to try using breakout groups for smaller conversations.

❑ Be Aware Of Your Mood

Especially if your energy as a facilitator or speaker is dependent on seeing or hearing your participants, be aware of your mood. Let's say you tell a joke, but you only hear silence. This may make you feel like no one thought it was funny, but it could just be that the participants were on mute or had their cameras off. How you intentionally draw people to turn on cameras and mics can make an impact on your energy levels and mood throughout the whole training or workshop. You may have to work extra hard to stay energetic if everyone is keeping their cameras off.

❑ Make The Learning Experience Comfortable And Meaningful

Listen carefully and look into the camera so participants feel like you are looking at them. Check in on body language cues, hear how participants are talking, and watch the chat. As an online facilitator and leader, ensure that your support teams feel their learning experiences are comfortable and meaningful.

❑ Watch Out For 'Resting' or 'Figuring It Out' Face

Watch out for your resting or 'figuring it out' face. It could shift participants' engagement or mood. So, keep your energy up and smile when appropriate.

❑ Think About Problem Attitudes

Think about Problem Attitudes, or issues when you facilitate online, and then unpack *why* this is happening and *how* you can alter the experience. This will also help to not dampen your energy during the learning event.

❑ Pause

Have you ever felt that you were interrupting someone online when you did not intend to? Sometimes, there are delays, which is why we cannot all sing together—it does not sound good. Give a brief pause after someone else has spoken before you talk. This shows good listening and helps reduce 'interruption.' We are all learning in the context of online communication. Pause often to ask if there are questions, especially since you may not be able to see everyone if they don't have their cameras on.

❑ Be Comfortable

Be comfortable. Online meetings or workshops can be the best of both worlds with not having to travel, but also getting the opportunity to collaborate and build community with a group. Your comfort level can set the tone for others. DON'T complain about how hard it is to learn online or the frustrations of technology. Yes, you want to be honest, but don't focus on something that you DON'T want your participants to focus on. This will come through on evaluations. Set the tone to be positive and understanding.

❑ Consider How Your Participants Feel

As a facilitator and leader, consider how your participants feel, especially when they don't like to be on camera. We show up for meetings prepared to see people. However, online meetings with a camera and mic may be new experiences for some people. Ensure that your participants feel comfortable and know what to expect.

❏ Build Up The Opening Energy

Building up the energy when opening a meeting or training is an important element for a leader online. One way to begin a meeting with positive energy is to share music as people enter the online meeting. Use different tempos of music depending on the mood and tone of the meeting. Another way to build up the energy is to consider mailing out an experience box ahead of time and ask everyone to open the box at the beginning. You can include treats, snacks, engagement props and more.

❏ Decide Who Will Be In The Spotlight

Depending on the platform you are using, decide if you want the main speaker, another facilitator, or yourself to be spotlighted. This can make you the main speaker view for everyone, instead of your participants seeing all the video tiles or gallery view. You can decide if this fits your context, tone, and learner/participant experience, and if this is needed for the replay recording.

❏ Take Time For Breaks

Energy for yourself and your participants can include the need for breaks. Sometimes, people refer to these as Bio Breaks so that participants don't miss any of the content. If your platform has an 'Away' notification, encourage people to use this. This way you know when people return.

❑ Have An Energizer Activity After Breaks

When you return from a break or self-study portion, include an energizer activity, and definitely use the engagement tools your platform provides. Using the reaction tools (i.e. the green checkmark) to double-check that everyone is back is a good option.

❑ Think About Your Participation Method

The way you call on or ask individuals to participate can impact the energy or enthusiasm of the group. You can start by asking people to type in chat or raise their virtual hand if they have the answer to your question. It's at that point that you can then call on someone to come onto the mic to tell you more. Provide warm engagement opportunities and not cold invites (i.e. naming someone), especially when a person may not be ready to come onto their mic at that moment.

❑ Consider Music

Music when you are coming back from breaks or a self-study is another option to maintain participants' engagement.

Consider if you want the music to be softer for the last ten seconds before the break is over or if you want exciting music to set the tone for the next part of the learning experience. It's also important to make sure that the music you are using is licensed to you or royalty-free, especially when you plan to record the event.

❑ **Don't Let Low Energy Become A Barrier To The Learning**

Be intentional about your energy and also about managing your participants' energy. Don't let low energy become a barrier to learning.

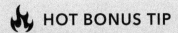 **HOT BONUS TIP**

Encourage participants to turn on their 'away' feature, if the platform you are using has this option. When people return from a break, ask people to turn off that notification and/or give you a green checkmark. It's good to double check who is back 'in the room,' especially before you place people in breakout rooms. Otherwise, you may not realize that someone isn't back at their desk yet.

CHAPTER FIVE

Promise: Your Goals Moving Forward

Your promise on what you will do moving forward can be the most important decision or step in online facilitating. This chapter about your promise isn't just a conclusion or recap, but an intentional aspect to your planning and goal evaluation. Your promise can be part of your goal setting as you continue to turn audience members into participants. Your intention may be to bring in more people, or improve evaluations. Whatever outcomes you are looking for, your promise to learn and improve or to try new things is part of the process. Your promise should also consider what you want to get out of being an online facilitator. Your intention or promise also helps you connect with your participants because they can feel that you really care about their learning experience, even if you're not formally telling them. To help, I've included below specific quick tips that you can choose to implement for your next event or workshop.

Promise In Practice – The Bored Board Chair

During a board meeting, when we were in the time of in-person meetings, a person was giving a presentation to the group. I noticed the board members starting to look around, and then fidget with their papers. She didn't appear to be listening. The presenter didn't have any visuals and was just talking in a normal tone. When the next presenter started, they included slides with visuals and interactive questions. There was an excitement for the material from the speaker and they were passionate about the topic. The board members were taking notes and engaged with the interactive discussion the speaker was leading. This can happen in the online space, too, and I often reflect on the difference in attention to each speaker. I like to think of those board members when I create my presentations and I have made the promise to try to engage the person who can easily tune out. My goal is always to turn an audience into participants.

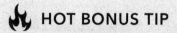 **HOT BONUS TIP**

When you are creating training materials, consider how they would work in different contexts, in-person, online, hybrid or different virtual platforms. If you have adaptations of your activities ready, you are able to easily shift if a last-minute change occurs.

Promise In Practice – The Forced Shift

Sometimes, when people are forced to work on a new platform, there is resistance. I was producing for a fantastic facilitator, and they preferred to work on the platform that they were most comfortable in. The platform we were using provided additional tools for engagement. However, their client group was used to another platform. Unfortunately, when their host was providing some words of welcome at the beginning of the session, they began to complain about the platform. This was not a great start to the learning experience. Beginning with a negative tone does not set up everyone for learning success. Keeping in mind that if a group is resistant to the change of a different learning platform, you may need to manage complaints and negative comments. In this case, setting up the chat to be with the hosts and co-hosts only, and not with everyone, is a bonus tip that you will find helpful.

 What To Promise Yourself As An Online Facilitator

❑ Keep Learning

Keep learning and exploring! This is part of the creative process and keeps your content fresh, accessible and engaging. Start with the tools you have and grow from there. Technology keeps changing. Therefore, your skills will keep growing. Plus, if you have to shift again, to the hybrid audience, remember you can do this, too!

❑ Know Your Tools

Get to know your tools and platform! You can do more when you are curious, so explore and play in the virtual space. There are many ways to interact with your participants. Hint: If there are three dots, or a menu that says more, click it and find out what it can do.

❑ Use Your Tools

Use the tools from the platform, such as polls, chat, annotation (i.e. writing on a whiteboard), and breakout rooms. This is even more important online so people do not feel that the meeting or training is a one-way, passive, listening experience.

❏ Have A Call To Action

Provide a call to action at the end of the session as a way to apply the learning. Pick one item that participants can try out as soon as possible so they remember what they learned. A call to action can be an engagement activity, too. For example, you can use the chat or a white board/ slide and annotation, depending on the platform you are using. Ask people to type their plans on applying the learning. Maybe include how and when, if you want to make it a SMART intention.

❏ Pay Attention To The Details

It's all about the details! Creating a timeline for your online event, training or meeting is essential. Yes, you can be flexible and respond to the needs of your participants, but a plan is key. You may want to include an evaluation section towards the end of your event so that you can improve some details in the future.

❏ Communicate The Little Things

Communication is what makes a learning experience great. With the time it takes to get into breakout groups, giving a reminder of how much time is left and then bringing everyone back together takes a few moments—just like it would in person. Consider the flow and steps it takes for the new context, or ask someone who can support you plan the learning experience. Providing the page number of a handout or resource, verbally and then typing it in chat, can help your participants to catch up, if they were distracted. Communicating the little things can prevent interruptions and help someone to not be embarrassed if they had to step away briefly.

❏ Adapt To Using Multiple Screens

Two monitors does help, but there is also a learning curve to switching from what you know. You may need to swap presenter view (slide show) to ensure that your participants are seeing the slides and not your notes. However, two monitors also allow you to see your participants, the chat and your slides. This may be a better experience for you, and therefore, it may be a better experience for your participants because you are acknowledging the chat and other aspects you might have not been paying attention to before.

❏ Engage

Promise yourself to make your live events and online training engaging and interactive for both you and your participants. If you are engaging a hybrid audience, with some people in-person and some online, continue to promise to not forget to engage those in the virtual context. Sometimes, keeping everyone on their own digital device is the best way to intentionally engage everyone equally.

❏ Work In Bite-Sized Pieces

Create meetings and learning experiences in bite-sized pieces. Think about using less than 10 minutes to share a few points, or one main point, then a brief switch of gears. This could be a brief video (make sure to share the clickable link) or show a picture and share a story. Ask a question. Engage your audience to participate and not just sit back. Once you've gone through that piece of information, then you can move onto the next bite-sized learning activity.

❏ Try Something New

Try new activities and tools, and keep exploring! Don't get stuck, and then get bored, or be boring for your participants. This may be taking extra steps such as mailing out a surprise engagement box ahead of time, creating a new content resource, or including prizes.

❏ Use Breakout Rooms

Use breakout rooms to break up the learning experience and give a small group collaborative learning experience. This also helps your social learners. Be sure to give a lot of detailed instructions before sending people into breakout rooms, like how long they have, if they need to take notes and when and how to report back. If you are on a platform where instructions do not follow them into their breakout room, invite people to take a picture of the instructions. In this case, you may also want to have the instructions included in a participant manual or in the resources sent ahead of time.

❏ Add Variety

Promise to add variety to the learning experience you are designing and to engage a variety of learning needs and preferences. Think of this like layers or aspects that you are sprinkling in to engage the variety in your audience. Also consider the variety of how people like to communicate and learn (i.e. Howard Gardner's Multiple Intelligences).

❏ Make Things Fun

People *can* learn in most situations, but if they are bored, they may tune you out. Especially when shifting to the online context, people can start doing other things, such as checking and responding to emails. So, make sure to keep your event fun for your participants.

❑ Create Aha Moments

Ignite the light bulbs of your participants by helping them to create aha moments with intention. Build on what they know and respect your participants as adult learners.

❑ Layer Up Your Style

If you only facilitate in one style (i.e. lecture), then you only light up or foster engagement for the people in your audience that prefer to learn in that way. Consider layering your style with a variety of different elements to intentionally engage more people.

❑ Stretch Your Comfort Zone

People tend to facilitate in the way they like to receive information. Stretch your comfort zone and expand your engagement reach.

❑ Be Descriptive

Communication is learning. Describe the photo you're sharing for the content you are explaining. Consider a variety of accessibility needs and contexts. Someone may only be able to listen to the presentation since they are traveling.

❑ Give Alternative Options

A person who has limited use of their hands may not be able to use the Annotation tool, for example. Still, include the actions and activities that engage those learners who need this activity to pay attention, but offer alternatives for others, such as letting these participants participate using their mic. Also consider if someone's technology is not working, or if they're attending the event through the web browser and not the platform app. Be aware of accessibility and privilege. Every person's context may differ.

❑ Watch Your Pace And Consider Using Cues

Watch your pace and ensure that you are considering visual and auditory cues when giving directions. Don't just point to something people can read on a slide or handout, but say the workbook page number out loud and type it in chat. People are taking in a variety of stimuli, especially when learning online, and if working from home. There can be a slight interruption too.

❑ Be Diverse And Inclusive

The photos you pick, the people you interview, the visuals in your promo, training, workshop or event should represent a variety of people.

❏ Get Creative With Your Presentations

Give your PowerPoints, Slides and Presentations a make-over by limiting your text to only what's most important. Have condensed points on each slide and don't forget to get creative with what you're presenting. Have pictures, videos, and questions to keep participants engaged.

❏ Be Attentive When Recording

If you are recording a video of the event, be sure to introduce yourself and ensure there is a beginning and closing to the video, especially for the replay and for those that were not part of the meeting. If you are recording a podcast version, consider describing the visuals that will not be available to those only listening. In this respect, you can also say 'Thank you for joining me today" instead of "Thank you for watching or listening."

❏ Shift Your Perspective

Your attitude and tone at the beginning of an event can lead the direction of your audience's focus. If you or others start complaining about the technology and how hard it is, then it will likely be a more painful experience. If you are positive, supportive and understanding, while designing an engaging learning experience *with many of the tips in this book*, you will be setting up everyone for success! I understand that shifting your workshops and training materials online included challenges and learning curves, but remember how far you have already come!

❑ Shift Your Online Audience Into Participants

Shifting your audience into participants requires an intentional approach to creating and facilitating the learning experience journey. Start with steps before an event, consider the needs during the event, and follow up the event with details that will aid knowledge retention. You want people to remember your content and the value-packed experience so they will apply what they have learned.

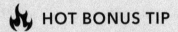 **HOT BONUS TIP**

The more you learn to play with a new engagement tool, the more you can get past the uncomfortable zone, and get into the creative zone.

CHAPTER SIX

Your Call to Action

You have come to the conclusion of the book, but this is not the end. I know, overall, each chapter makes up a long list of quick pro tips, but promise to start with one tip from each section, or focus on one section and a few quick tips first. Doing so will take your online facilitating to the next level, and you'll be able to engage with and gain more participants.

Start where you are and use what you have, but commit to continuing to grow. Build your events and workshops—and yourself—by choosing and implementing one quick tip at a time.

Planning is key! No matter the size of your group or the activities you want to share, it's good to plan ahead. This will ensure everyone has a good time and you're not scrambling to find links to send, and that document that one person can't find. Set up your online learning experience or event for success, so that everyone can have a fun, engaging and valuable time!

Adapt tips to fit your context. Do something, even if it stretches you a little bit! Promise yourself to add value to what you're presenting and turn an audience into participants. Add something into the promotion of your workshop that gets people excited. Add something to help prepare your participants and yourself for the next learning event. Don't forget the prelude time and how it can impact attitudes and attention. Remember, technology is always changing. All we can do is embrace it, but in regards to engagement in tech tools, remember to keep learning and stay curious.

You can do this! **You *are* doing this!** And you can continue to shift your workshops, meetings and presentations online and do a great job. You can shift attitudes, whether it's your own or someone you are working with, to be positive about the virtual context.

You can shift your audience to being open to learning how to navigate and participate online. The online shift for learning should not be passive, but an engaging experience.

It's good to have a call to action at the end of your training session or event. It's a way to encourage people to apply what they have learned. You could also build in a follow-up, if that fits.

So, what quick pro tips will you choose first? Take your pick and try one out today!

I welcome you to shift from this book to the QR codes below. They are bonus value-added tips, tutorials, and resources for you to keep going.

You'll find more free resources
on my Youtube page:

Ready to really become a Pro? Check
out my page for access to information,
courses and free resources:

101 QUICK PRO TIPS

For more information on these quick pro tips, feel free to go to their designated chapters.

Chapter 1: Promo

1. ❏ Bring People Into A Safe, Authentic Space
2. ❏ Incorporate Breaks & Snacks
3. ❏ Be Aware Of How Engagement Impacts Learning
4. ❏ Add A Time Zone To Your Promo Information
5. ❏ Make An Introduction Or Welcome Video
6. ❏ Find Out What Your Participants' Needs Are
7. ❏ Share Necessary Links And Have Your Participants Test Them Beforehand
8. ❏ Get Creative With Pre-event Promotion And Information
9. ❏ Create A Pre-Survey
10. ❏ Share Bite Size Tips
11. ❏ Remember Promotion Is More Than Marketing

Chapter 2: Preparedness

How To Prepare As A Facilitator

12. ❏ Know Being Prepared Makes All The Difference In Online Facilitating
13. ❏ Have Your Technology And Equipment Ready Ahead Of Time
14. ❏ Be Sure Your Internet Is Strong
15. ❏ Give Your Participants Instructions
16. ❏ Share And Discuss Expectations
17. ❏ Ensure Partnering Facilitators Are Prepared
18. ❏ Have Back-Up Plans Prepared
19. ❏ Prepare Resources For Your Participants
20. ❏ Include 'Clickable' Links
21. ❏ Make Sure Your Speakers Are Ready
22. ❏ Communicate With Your Team Or Partners
23. ❏ Create A Timeline Or Guide
24. ❏ Test And Update Your Technology
25. ❏ Record

How To Prepare Your Participants

26. ❏ Provide Support With Tools
27. ❏ Be Mindful Of Your Participants' Learning and Technical Conditions
28. ❏ Ask If Accessibility Or Learning Needs Are Required
29. ❏ Lay Down Ground Rules
30. ❏ Make Sure Events Get Added To Participants' Calendars

31. ❏ Add Reminders And Support Once Your Event Is Set Up
32. ❏ Send The Platform's Backup Phone Number
33. ❏ Make Sure Participants Have Their Documents

Chapter 3: Prelude

34. ❏ Add Details To The Waiting Room
35. ❏ Send Your Participants Friendly Messages
36. ❏ Decide If Participants Will Join Muted Or Unmuted
37. ❏ Have A Welcome Message Ready
38. ❏ Ask In The Chat About Closed Captioning
39. ❏ Set The Tone With Music
40. ❏ Let Participants In Early
41. ❏ Consider Turning Off The Waiting Room Once It Is Time To Start
42. ❏ Start With A Tech Check
43. ❏ Have A Navigation Slide
44. ❏ Screen Share Your Desktop
45. ❏ Consider Navigation Differences
46. ❏ Check In On Your Participants
47. ❏ Have Online Roundtable Introductions
48. ❏ Enable Follow Host Order
49. ❏ Make The Prelude As Inviting And Comfortable Online As It Would Be In Person
50. ❏ Have Fun, Relevant Warm-Up Activities
51. ❏ Have An Energizer Activity
52. ❏ Have A Virtual Background Icebreaker
53. ❏ Use The White Board Annotation
54. ❏ Think About Purpose, Process, and Payoff

55. ❏ Spotlight The Speaker
56. ❏ Consider The Details When You Set The Stage For The Learning Experience

Chapter 4: Presence

57. ❏ Be Intentional
58. ❏ Energy Is Key
59. ❏ Use Props
60. ❏ Make Eye Contact
61. ❏ Build Connection
62. ❏ Communicate
63. ❏ Be Present
64. ❏ Be Aware Of Your Mood
65. ❏ Make The Learning Experience Comfortable And Meaningful
66. ❏ Watch Out For 'Resting' or 'Figuring It Out' Face
67. ❏ Think About Problem Attitudes
68. ❏ Pause
69. ❏ Be Comfortable
70. ❏ Consider How Your Participants Feel
71. ❏ Build Up The Opening Energy
72. ❏ Decide Who Will Be In The Spotlight
73. ❏ Take Time For Breaks
74. ❏ Have An Energizer Activity After Breaks
75. ❏ Think About Your Participation Method
76. ❏ Consider Music
77. ❏ Don't Let Low Energy Become A Barrier To The Learning

Chapter 5: Promise

78. ❑ Keep Learning
79. ❑ Know Your Tools
80. ❑ Use Your Tools
81. ❑ Have A Call To Action
82. ❑ Pay Attention To The Details
83. ❑ Communicate The Little Things
84. ❑ Adapt To Using Multiple Screens
85. ❑ Engage
86. ❑ Work In Bite-Sized Pieces
87. ❑ Try Something New
88. ❑ Use Breakout Rooms
89. ❑ Add Variety
90. ❑ Make Things Fun
91. ❑ Create Aha Moments
92. ❑ Layer Up Your Style
93. ❑ Stretch Your Comfort Zone
94. ❑ Be Descriptive
95. ❑ Give Alternative Options
96. ❑ Watch Your Pace And Consider Using Cues
97. ❑ Be Diverse And Inclusive
98. ❑ Get Creative With Your Presentations
99. ❑ Be Attentive When Recording
100. ❑ Shift Your Perspective
101. ❑ Shift Your Online Audience Into Participants

ACKNOWLEDGMENTS

Acknowledge that my knowledge is partnered with responding to my clients' questions, and my research to meet their needs.

To my book writing group who have walked this journey alongside me, you are all amazing!

To my co-workers (going way back) whom I worked with at our local library when I was a teenager, I know you understand how exciting this is!

To my instructors at Yorkville University, where I expanded my knowledge about Adult Education, you helped change the course of my career.

And to the incredible launch squad at Life to Paper Publishing, you are the team I needed to make this dream a reality. Thank you!

ABOUT THE AUTHOR

Patricia Regier is the Online Expert who's built a career on the belief that training doesn't have to be boring. Her debut book, The Online Shift: 101 Pro Tips for Online Facilitators, Workplace Trainers & Virtual Speakers teaches newcomers to the online space and seasoned professionals alike how to optimize their online presence and maximize engagement. Owner of Regier Educational Services, Patricia was focused online before online became every day. She's tried, tested and refined using the latest behavioral science, research and psychology to make sure your next online experience is a hit!

CPSIA information can be obtained
at www.ICGtesting.com
Printed in the USA
LVHW040132170622
721464LV00003B/425

9 781778 011153